COLOUR MY WORLD

Om KIDZ

An imprint of Om Books International

Om KIDZ | Om Books International

Reprinted in 2024

Corporate & Editorial Office
A-12, Sector 64, Noida 201 301
Uttar Pradesh, India
Phone: +91 120 477 4100
Email: editorial@ombooks.com
Website: www.ombooksinternational.com

Sales Office
107, Ansari Road, Darya Ganj
New Delhi 110 002, India
Phone: +91 11 4000 9000
Email: sales@ombooks.com
Website: www.ombooks.com

ISBN: 978-93-5276-669-7

Printed in India

10 9 8 7 6 5 4 3

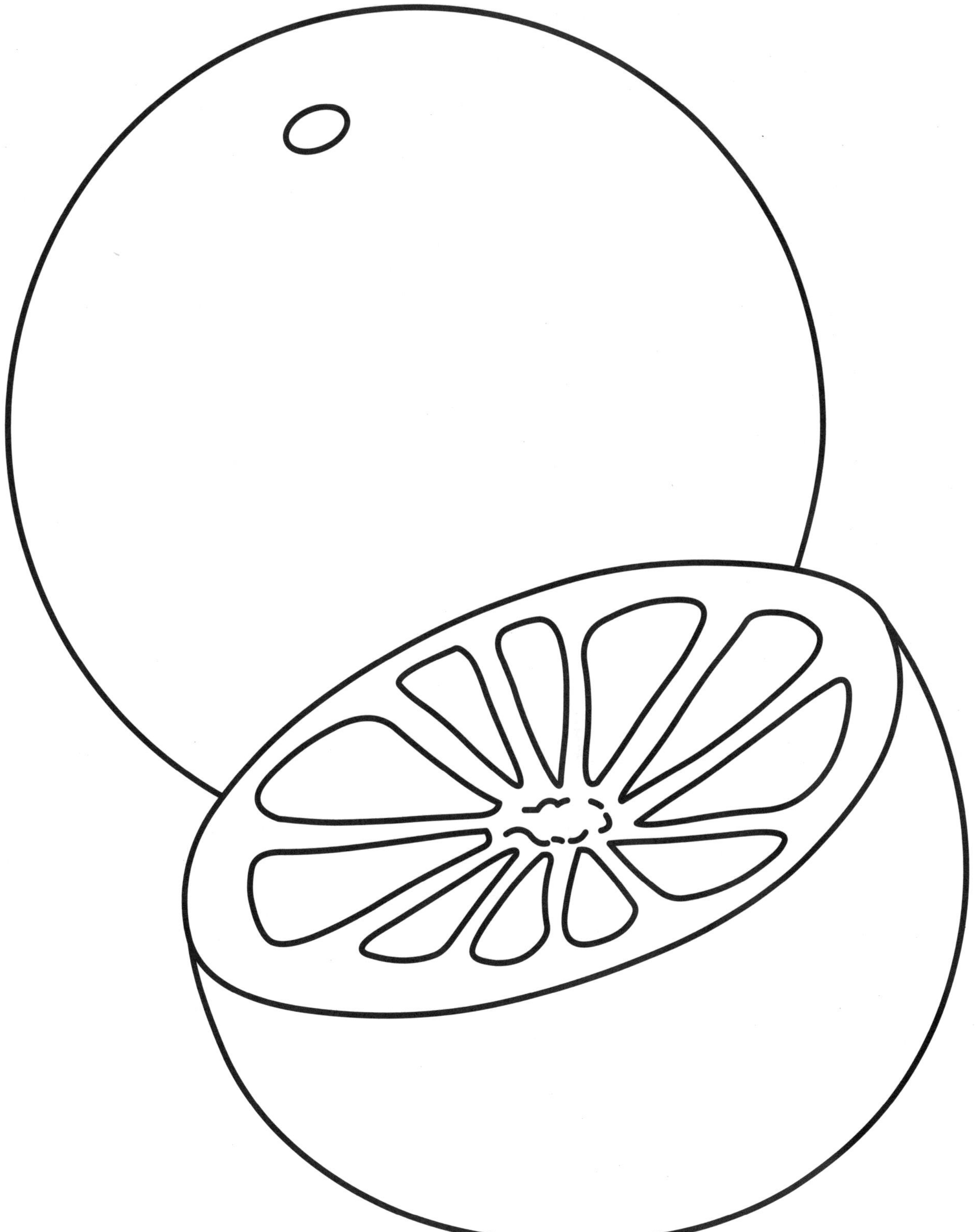

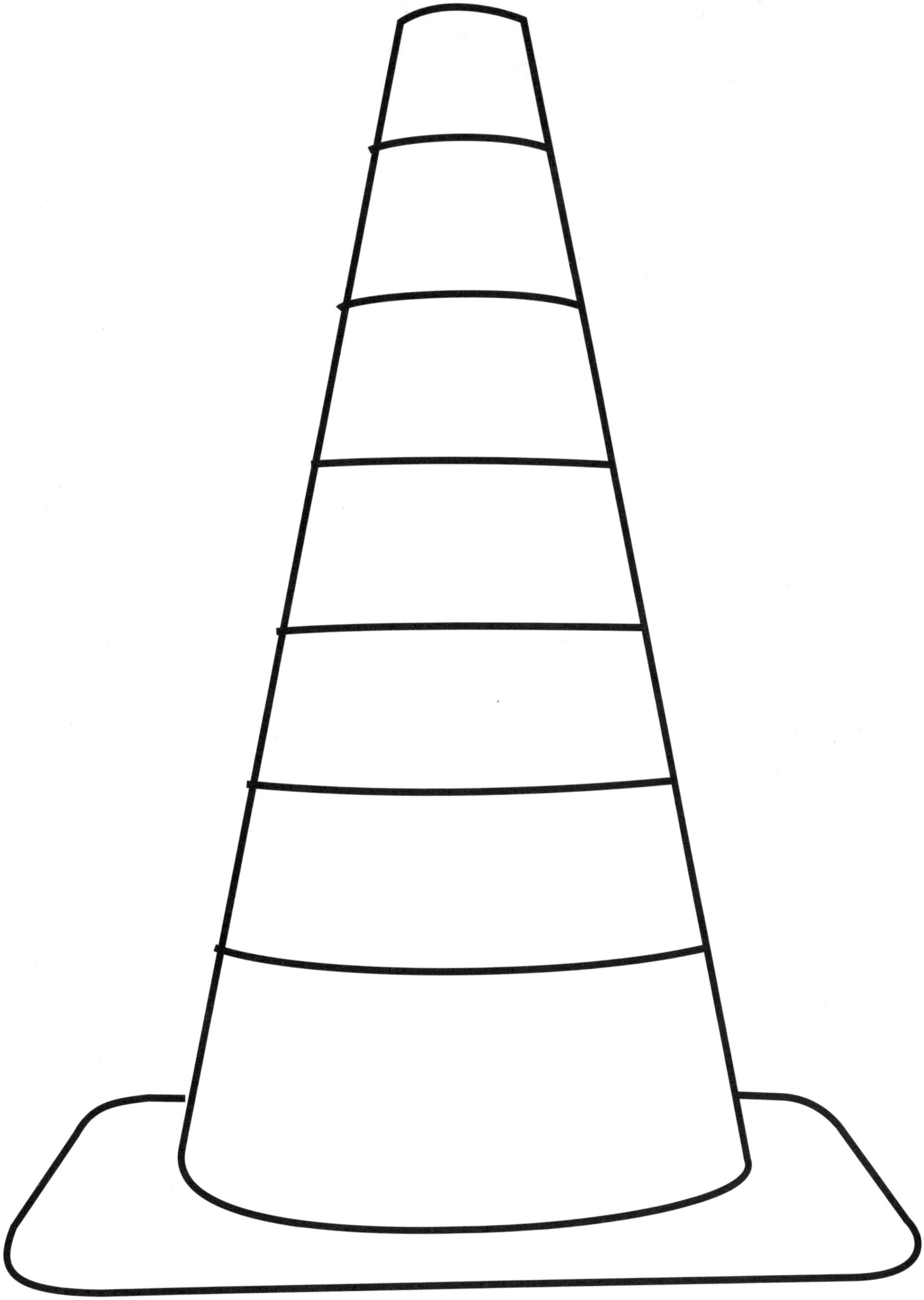

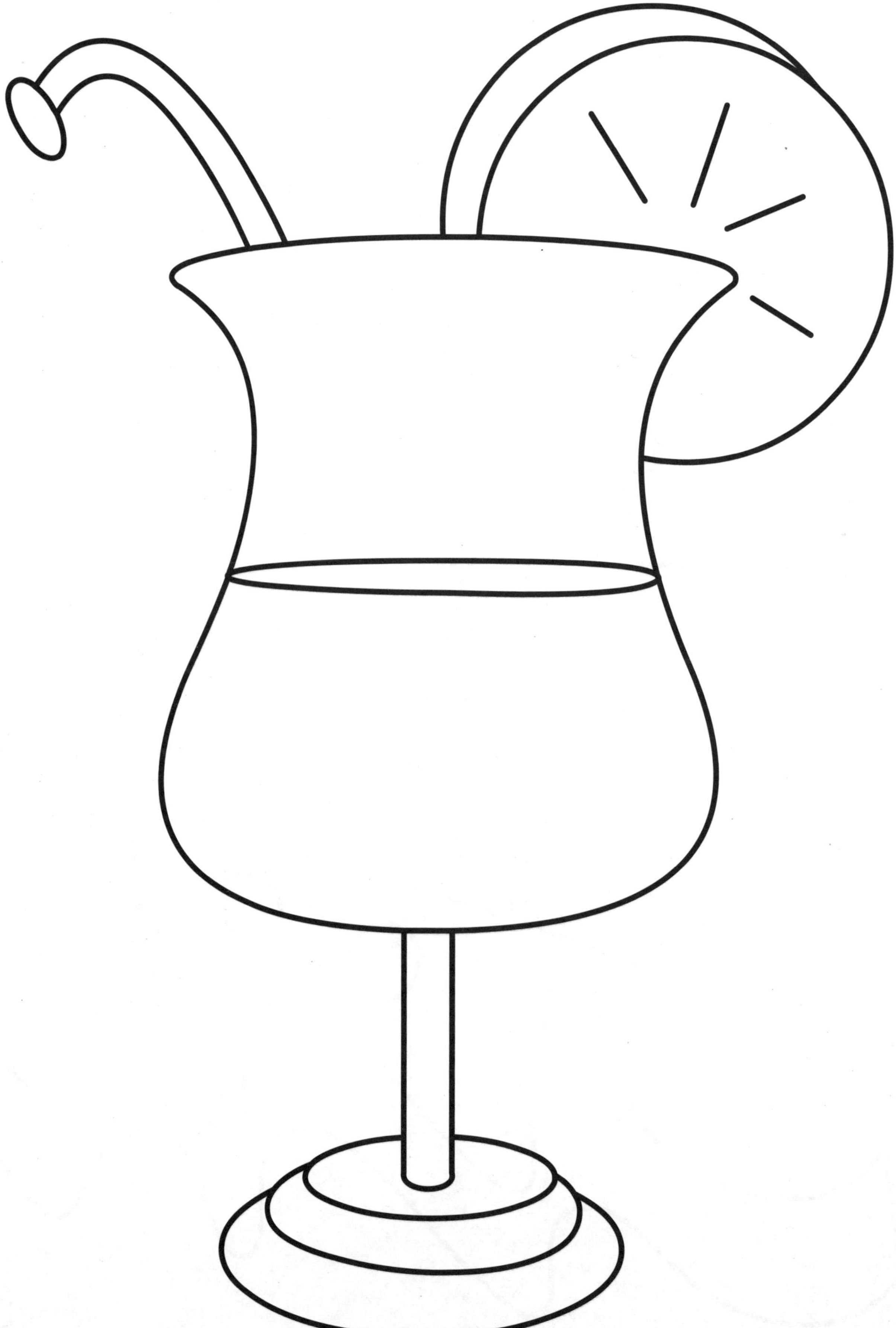

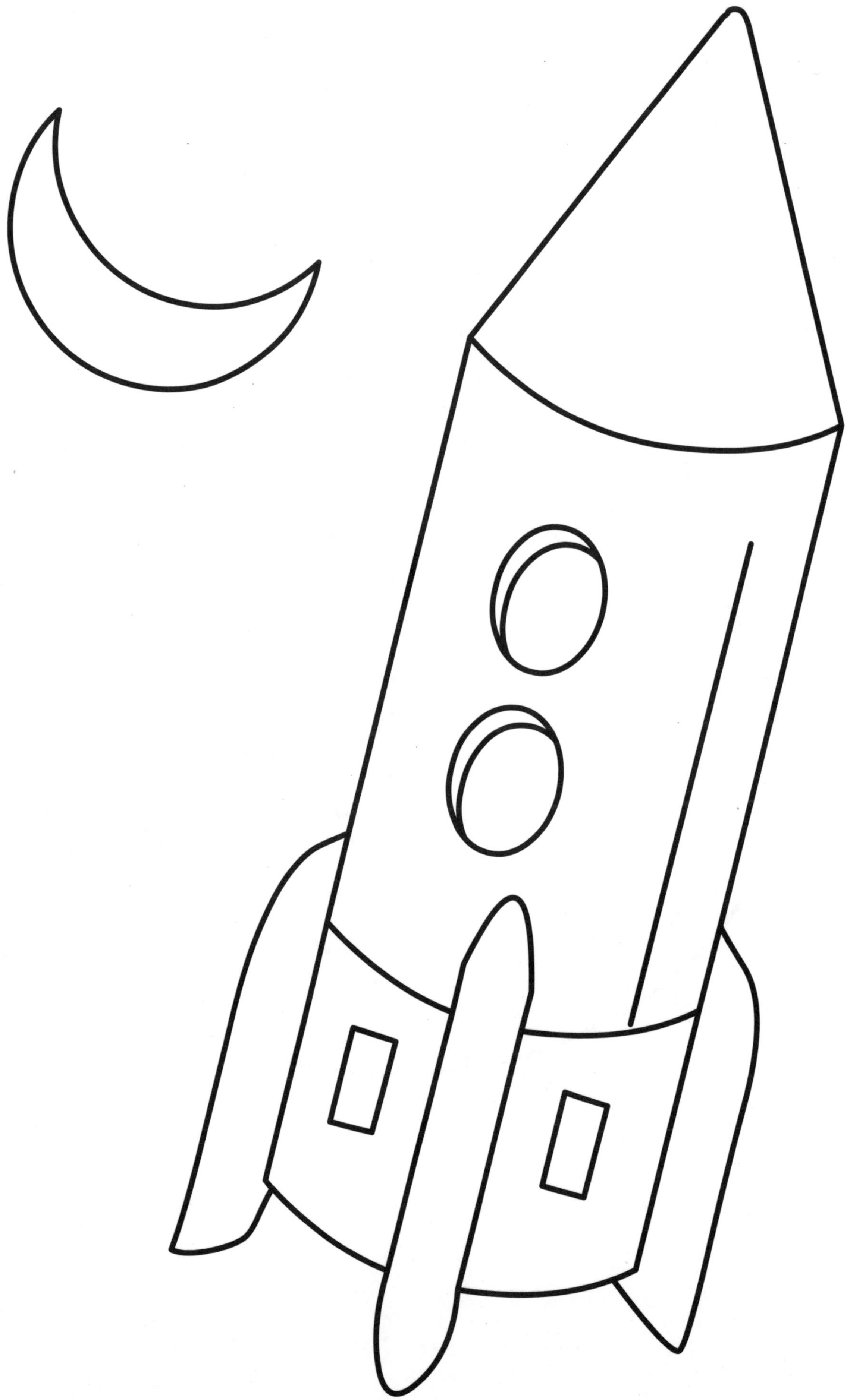

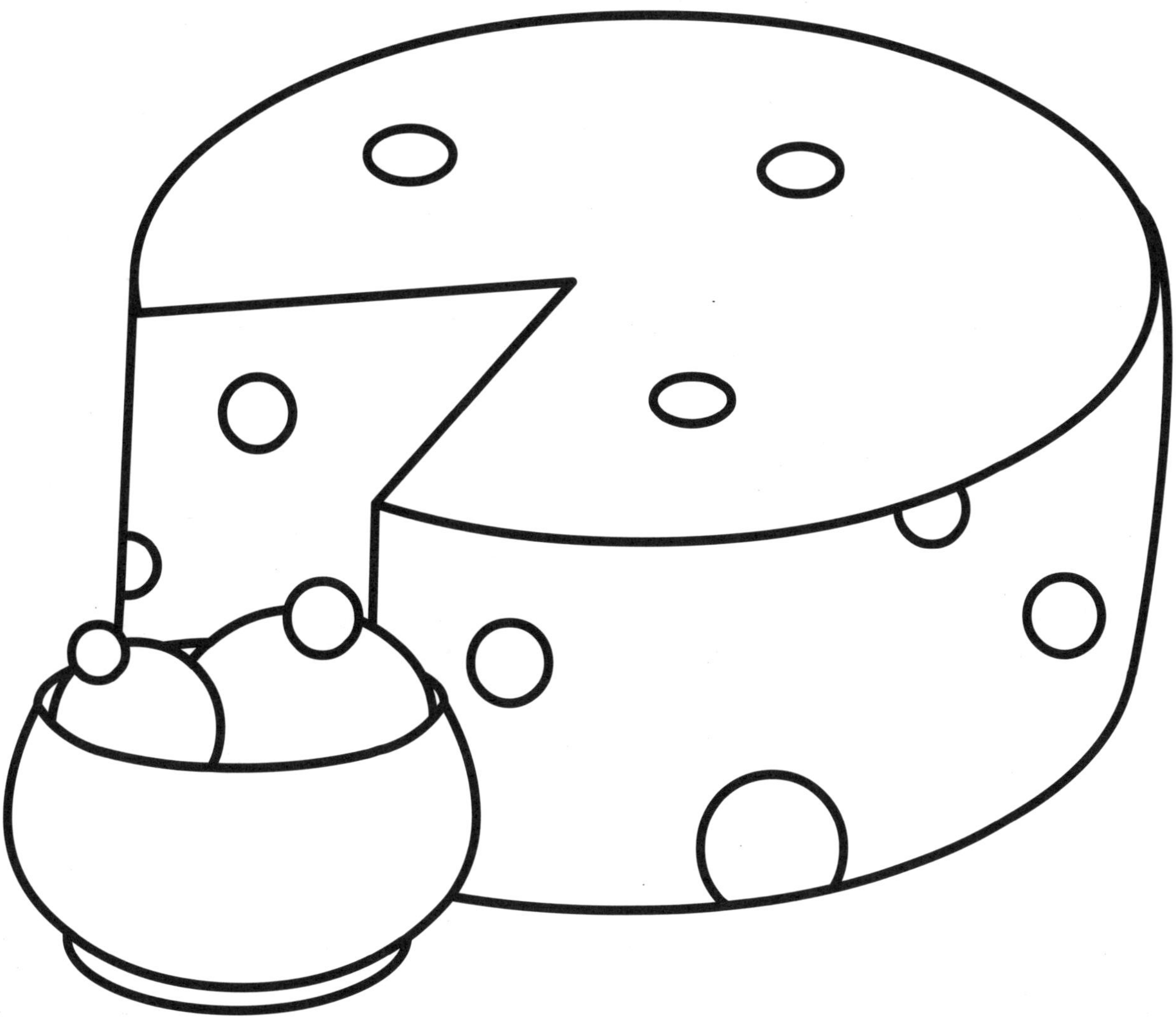

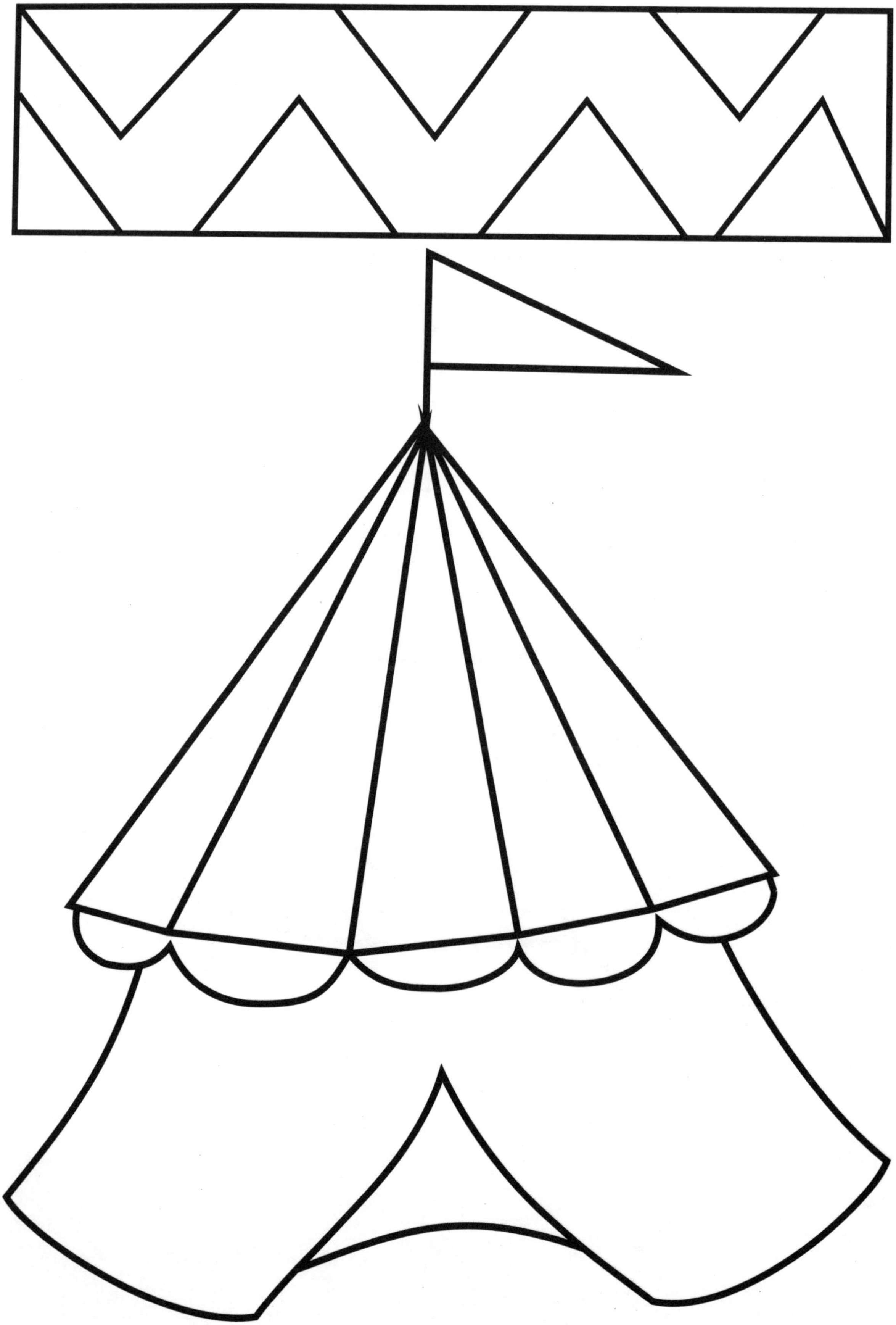

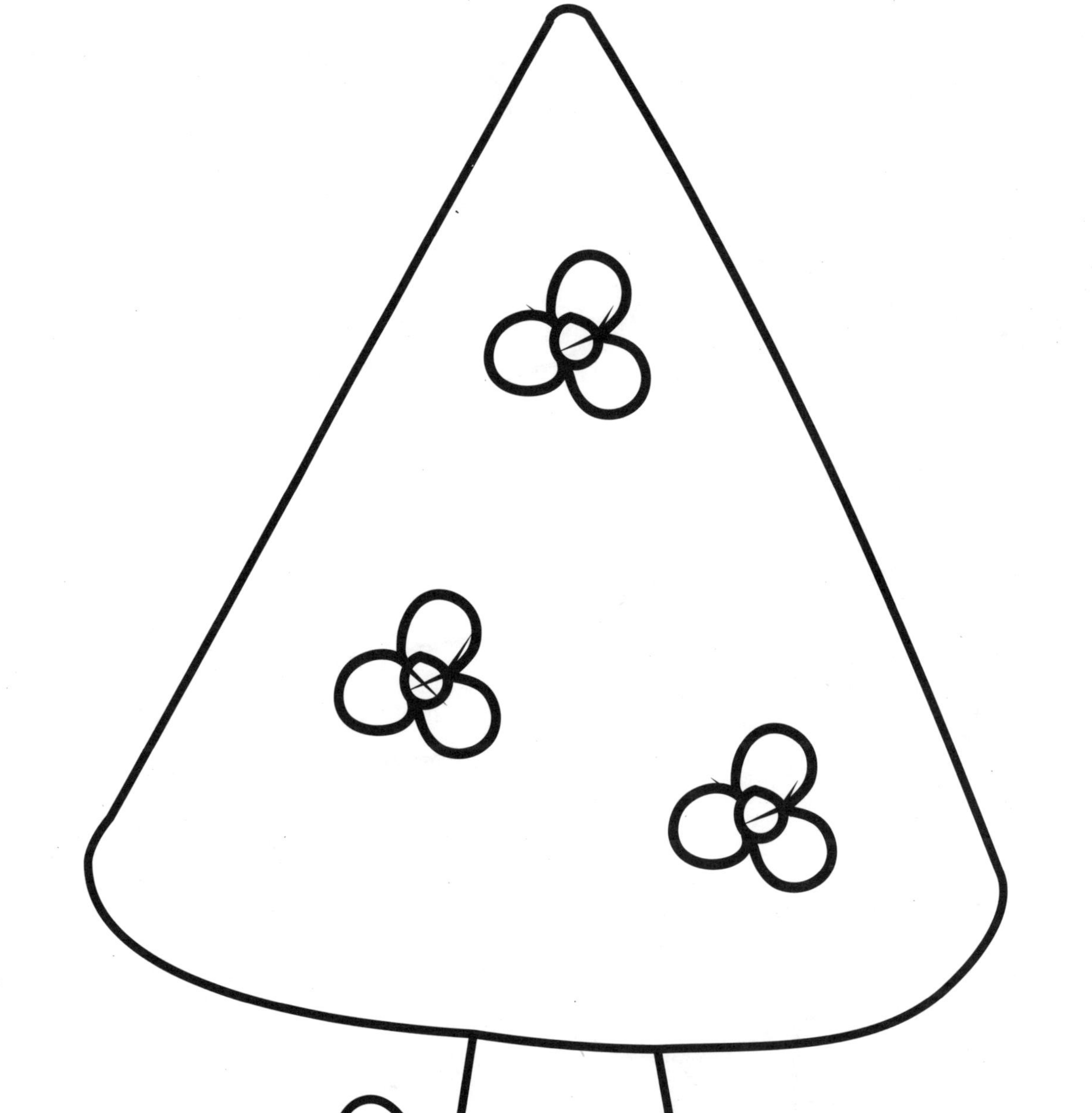

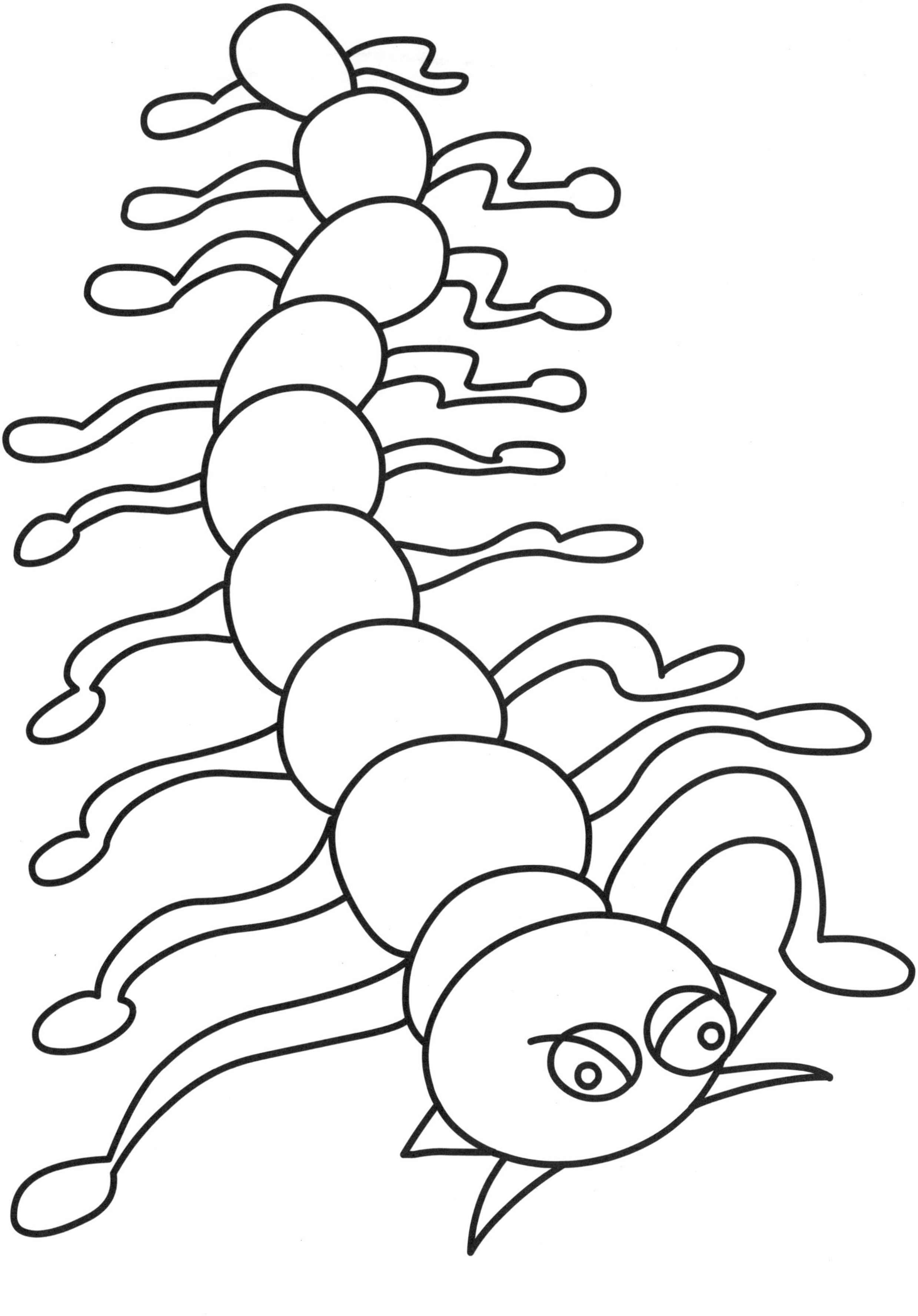

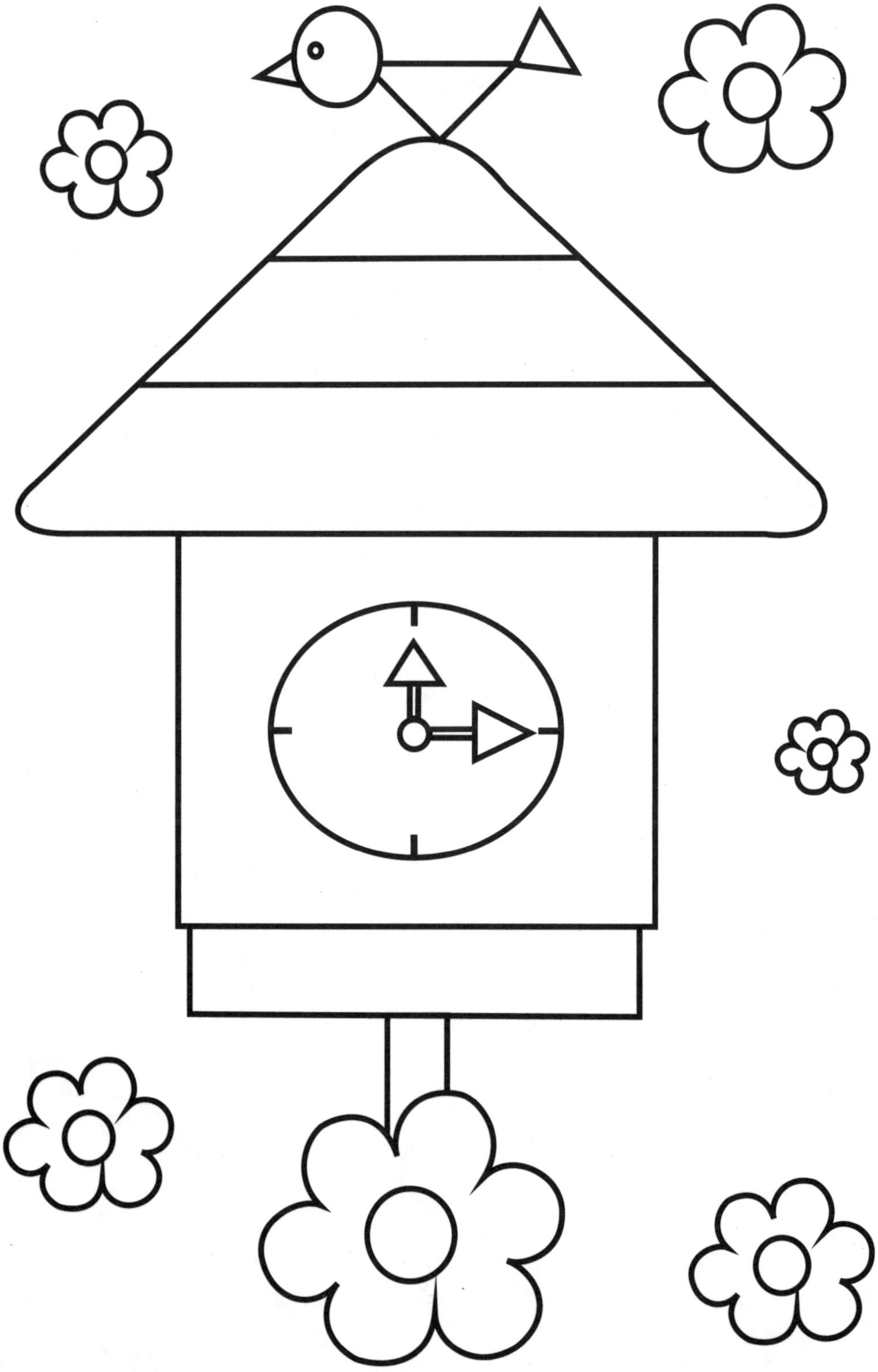

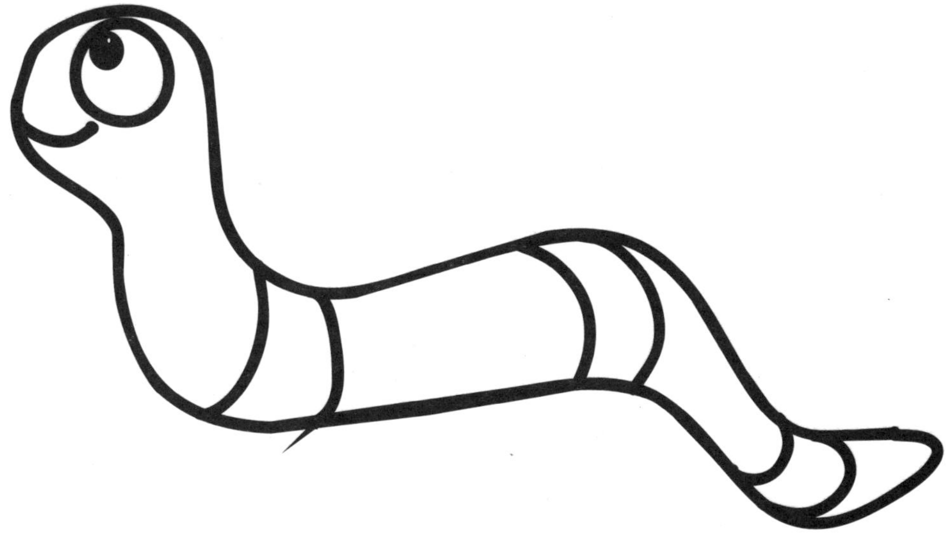

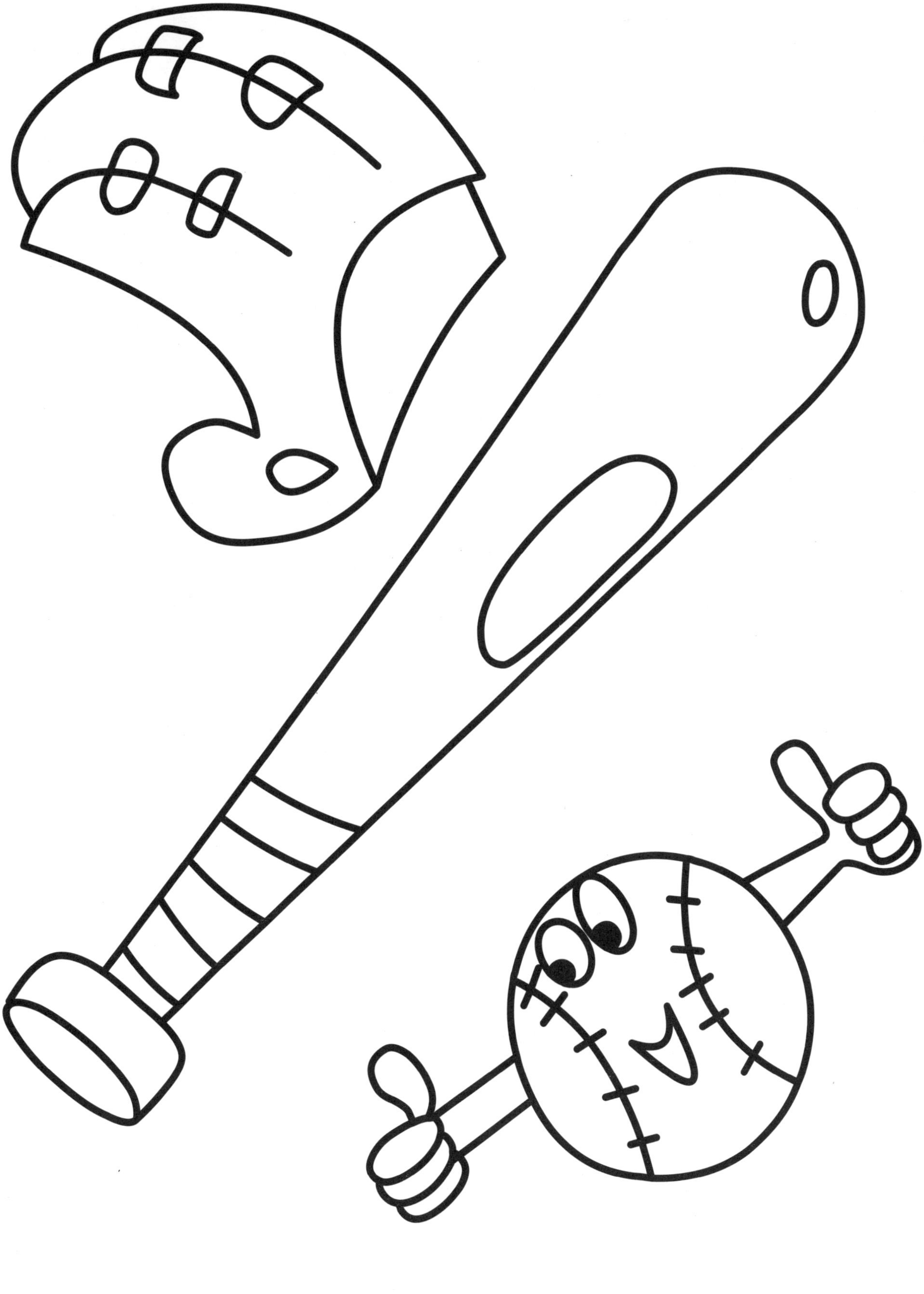

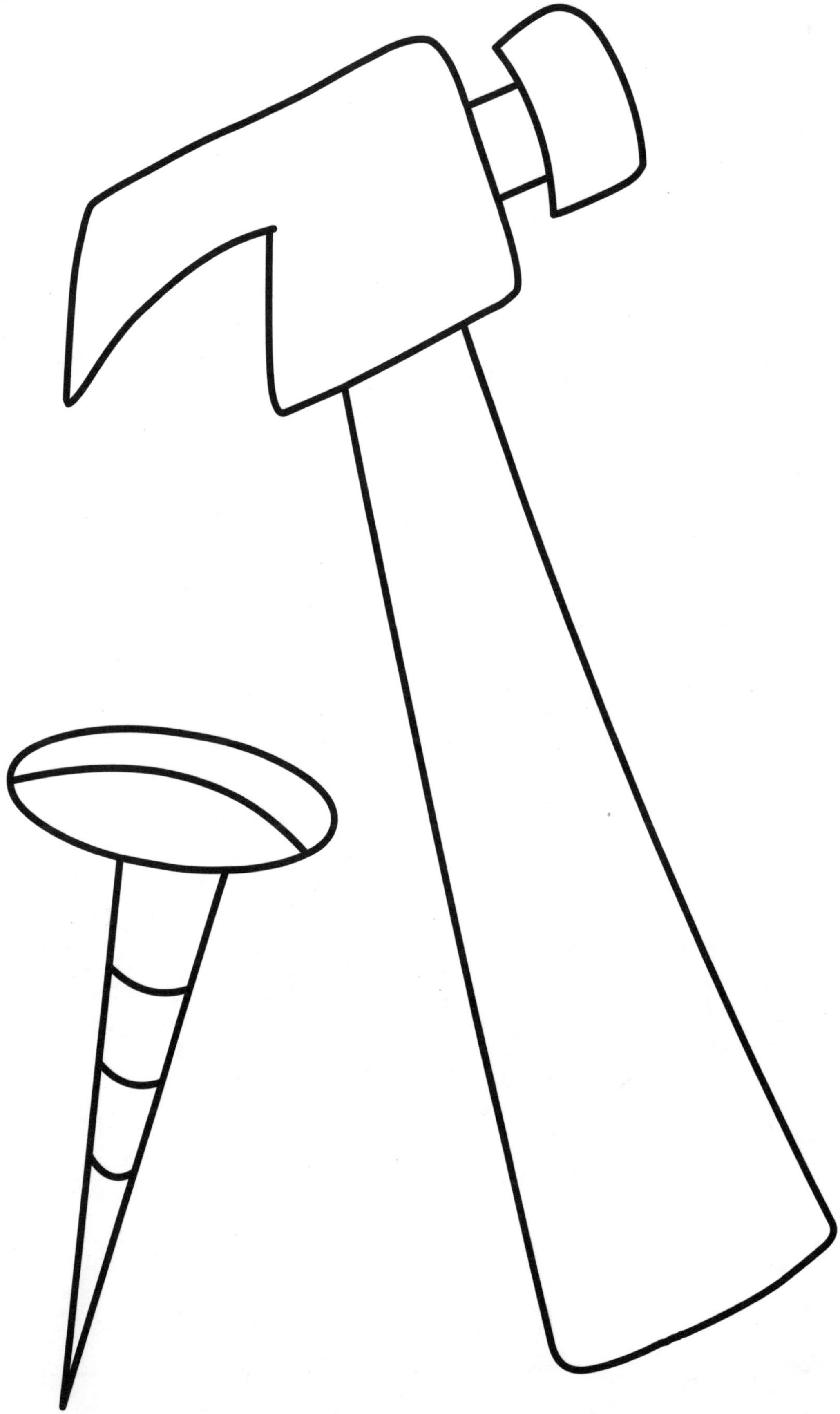

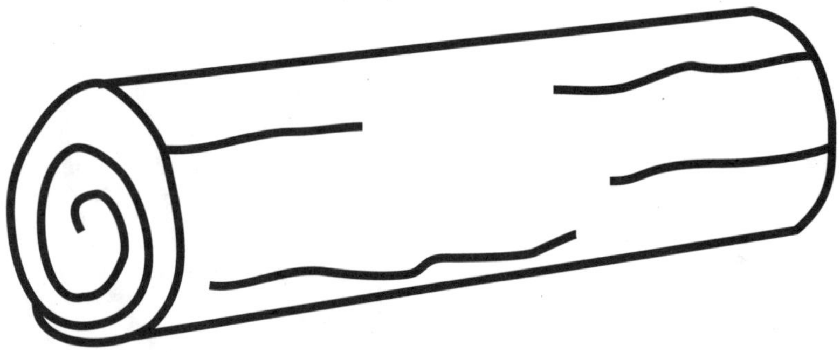

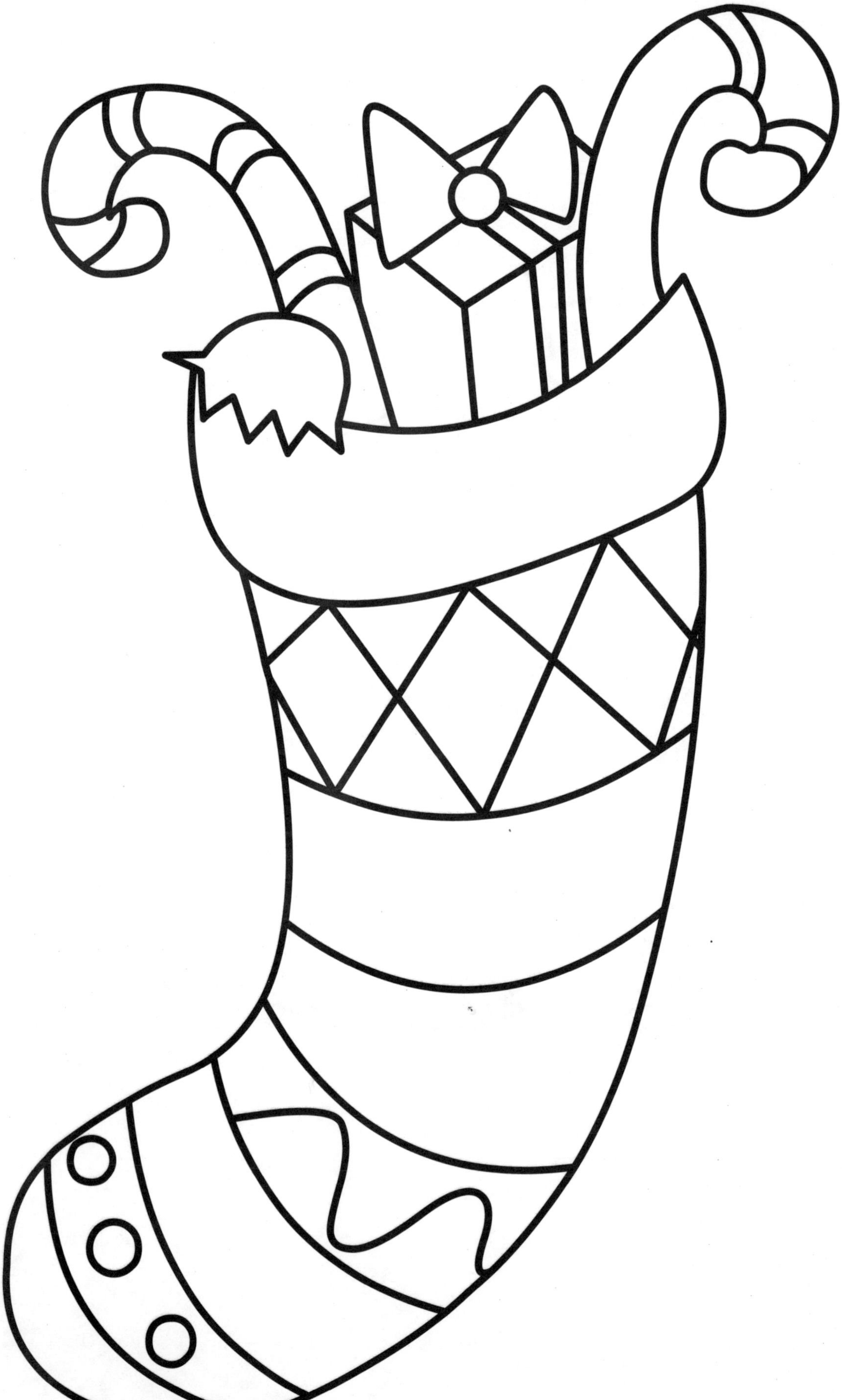

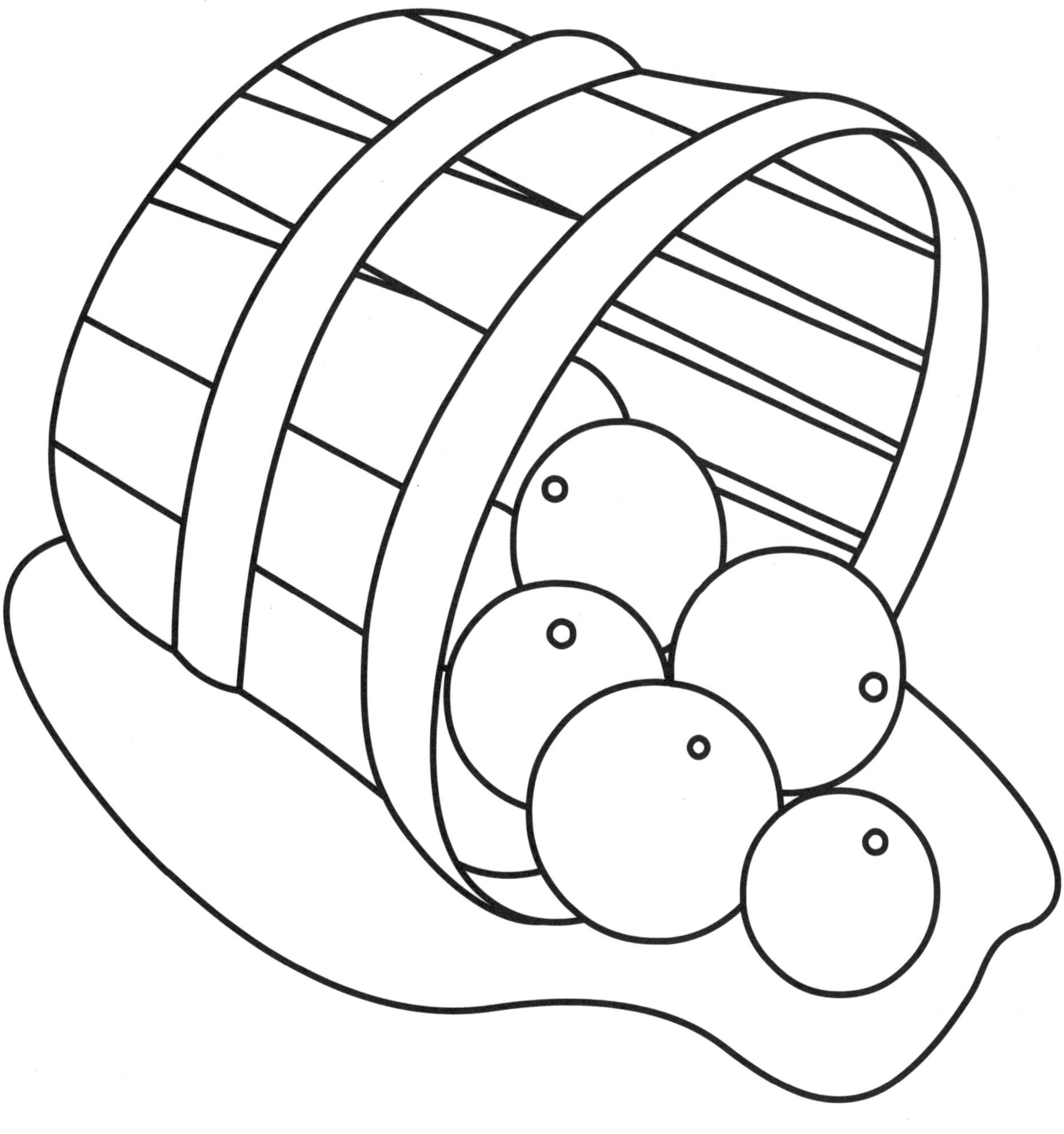

12
11
1
10
2
9
3
8
4
7
6
5

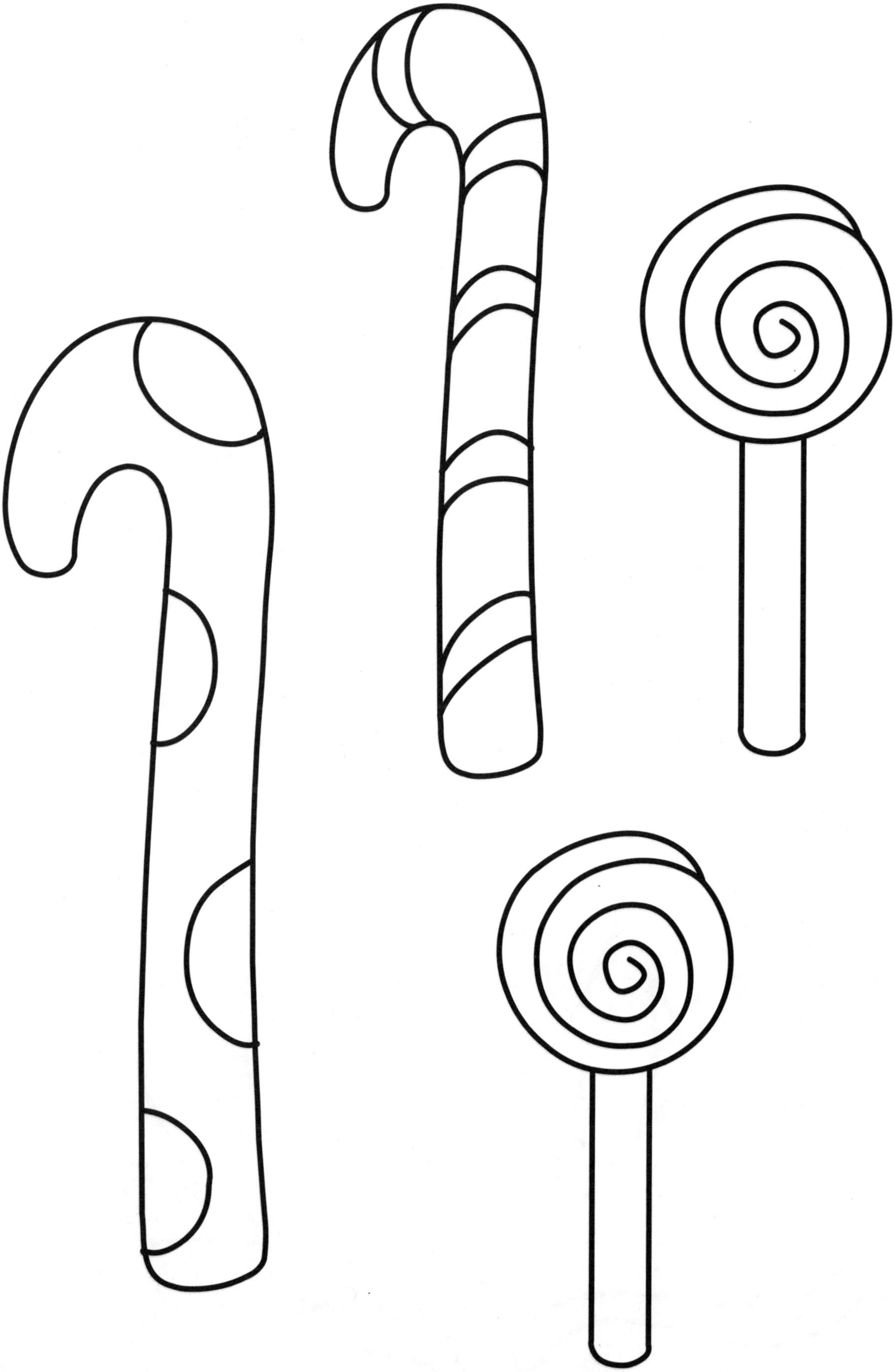

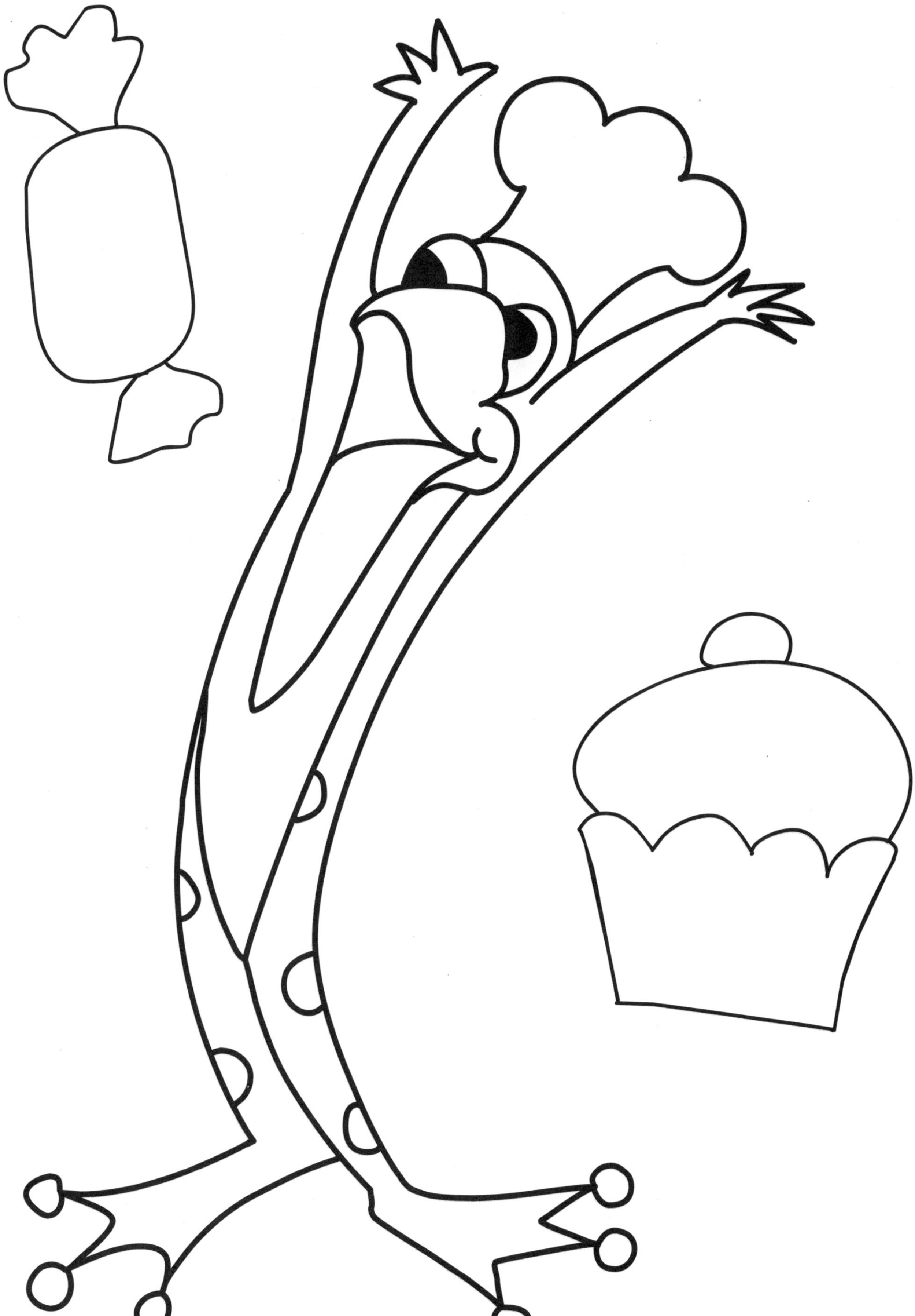

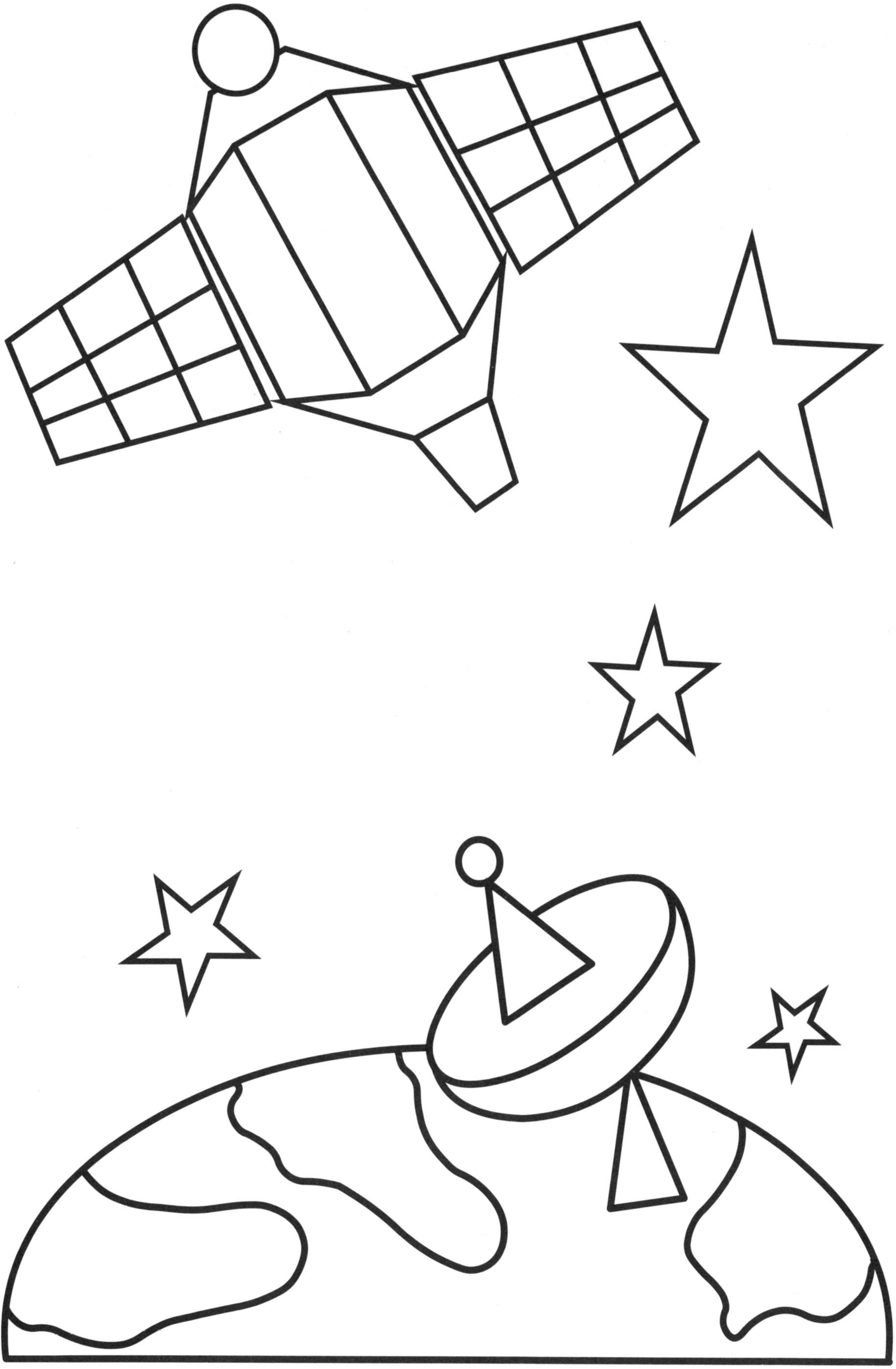

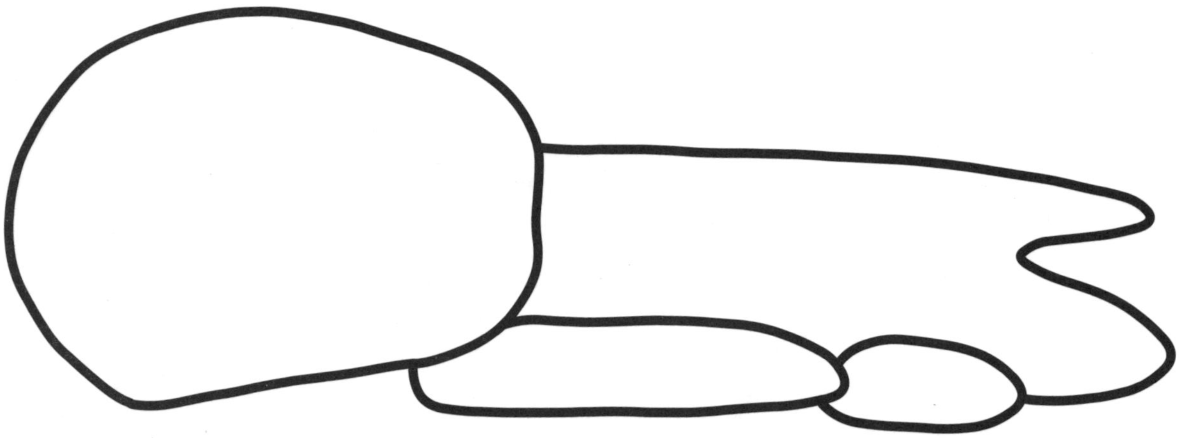

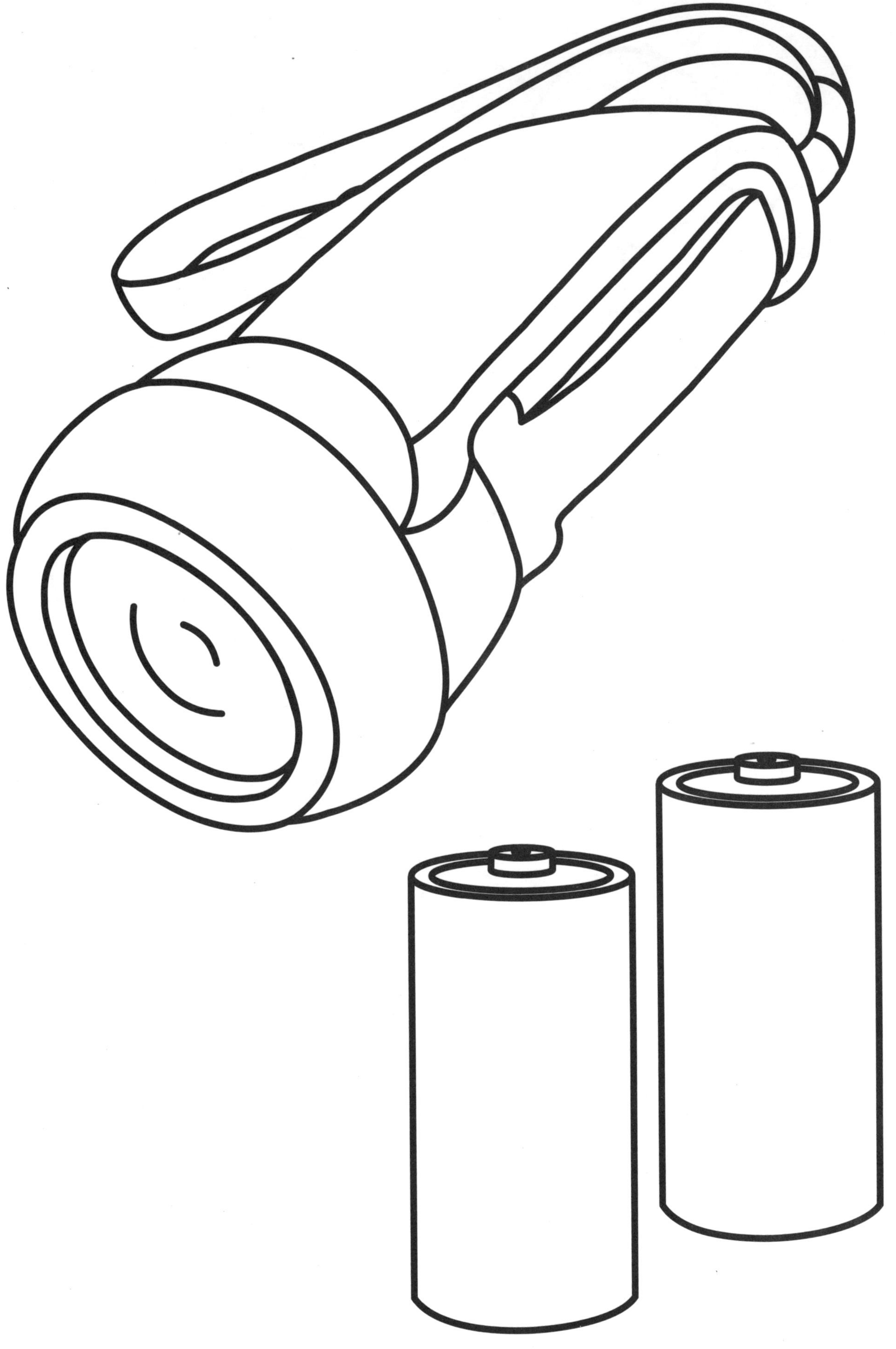

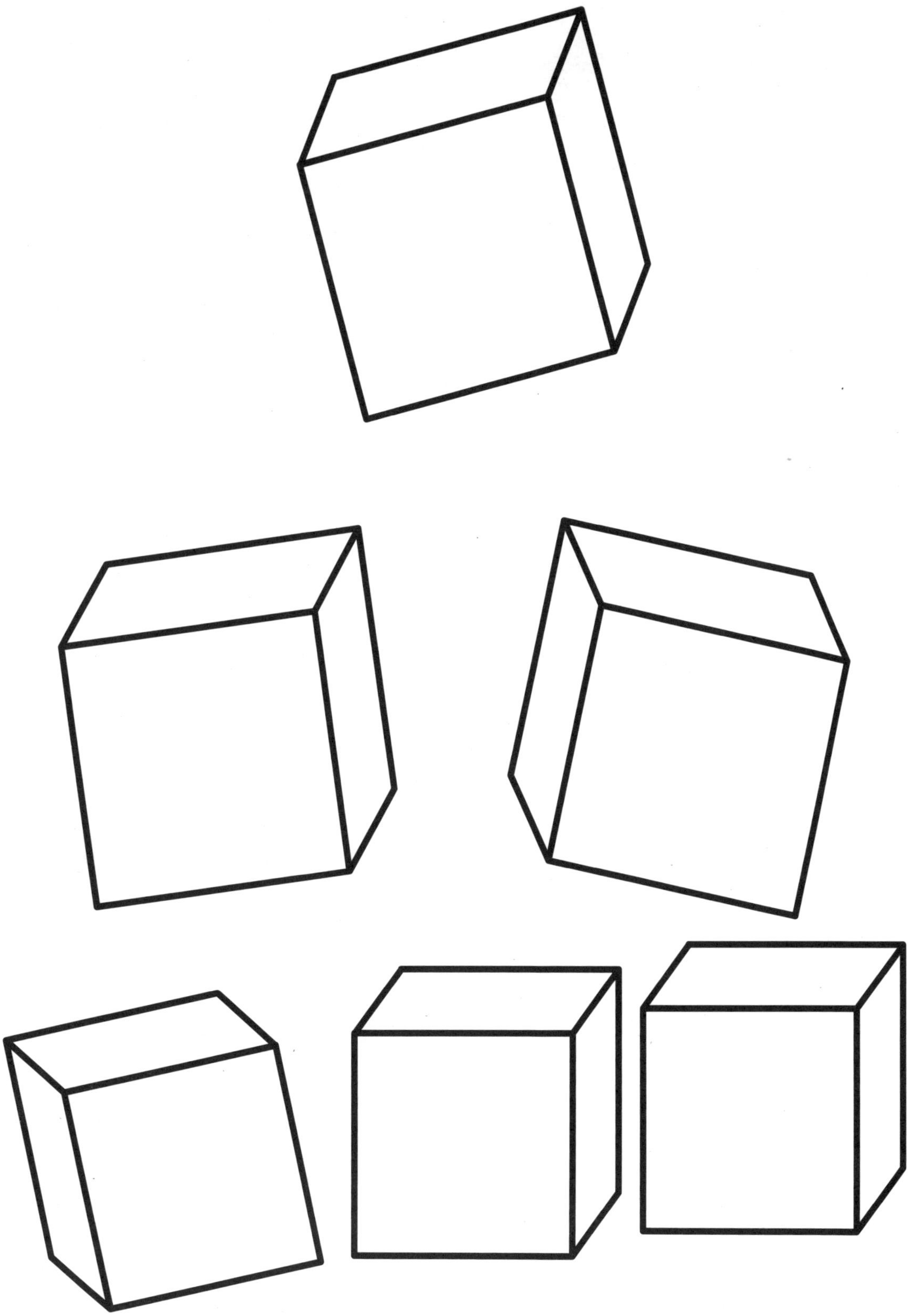

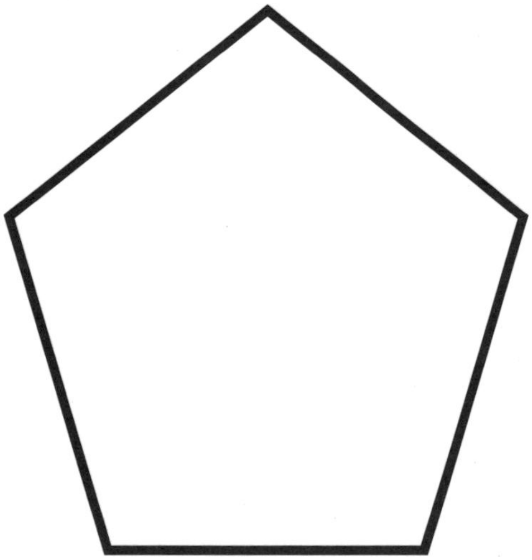

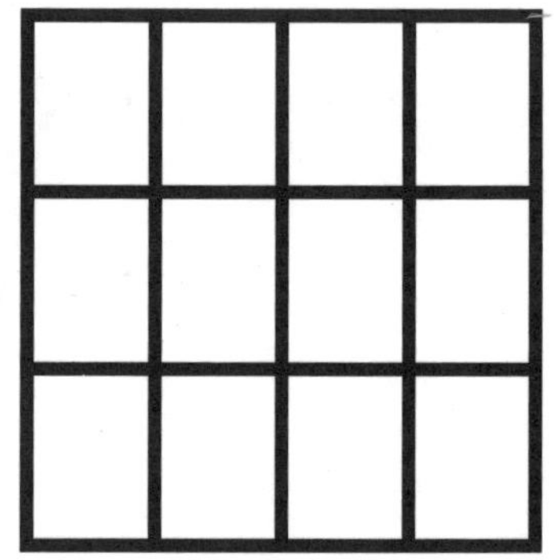

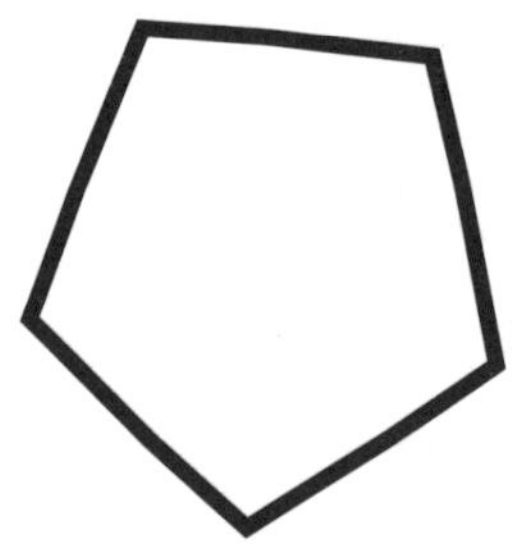

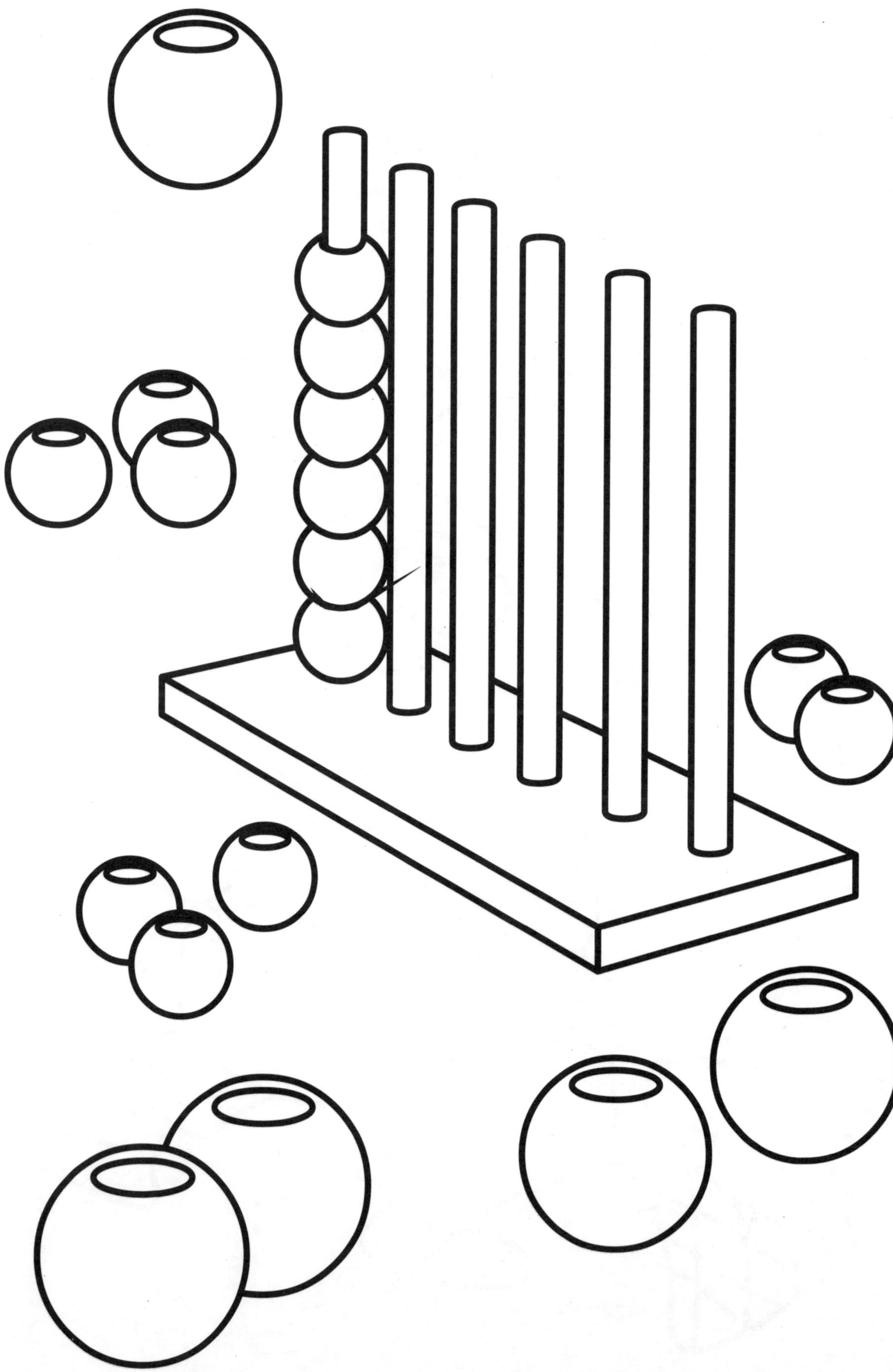